CONTENTS

Words that appear in in bold, **like this**, are explained in the glossary.

WHAT IS A RAINFOREST FOOD CHAIN?

The warm, moist River Amazon **basin** is home to the world's largest rainforest. Part the dense **vegetation** (plant life) and take a peek. Thousands of different plants and animals live here, between the damp ground and the treetops.

On the forest floor, a millipede munches a leaf. Soon a furry brown wolf spider inches closer. It traps the millipede and gobbles it up. Suddenly a brightly-coloured toucan leaves its treetop perch. Toucans mostly eat berries and seeds, but today it spies the wolf spider and glides down towards it. The toucan snatches the spider in its beak and swallows it whole.

When the toucan dies, **decomposers** such as **bacteria** will break down its body. Decomposers break down dead plant and animal material. This releases **energy** back into the water and soil. Soon other living things will take in that energy, and the process will begin again.

An orangutan crouches in the dense rainforest vegetation.

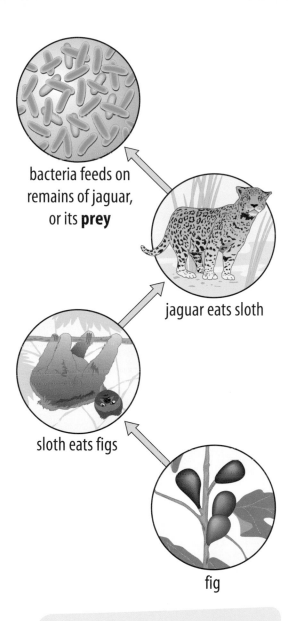

bacteria feeds on remains of jaguar, or its **prey**

jaguar eats sloth

sloth eats figs

fig

This food chain diagram shows how energy moves from one organism to another.

FOOD CHAINS

This process is called a food chain. A food chain shows how energy moves from one **organism** to another. An organism is any living thing. Energy moves from one living thing to another when one organism feeds on another.

Sometimes this process is shown using a food chain diagram. A food chain diagram has a series of arrows. The arrows show the flow of energy. Energy flows from the food to the animal that eats it. For example, in the rainforest food chain to the left, the arrows lead from the figs to the sloth, from the sloth to the jaguar, and so on.

Each link in a food chain is important. When something happens to one link, it affects the entire chain. Although humans have done much to harm rainforest food chains, they depend on them, too. It is important that humans start working to protect Earth's rainforests.

WHAT ARE THE PARTS OF A FOOD CHAIN?

Producers are plants. Plants use light energy from the Sun to produce food.

A **consumer** cannot make its own food. Consumers eat plants, animals, or both. There are three types of consumer. A **primary consumer**, or **herbivore**, eats only plants. **Carnivores** eat only animals. **Omnivores** eat both plants and animals. Carnivores and omnivores are also called **secondary consumers**.

Decomposers help release energy for producers. This frees up energy for the food chain process to continue. Decomposers feed on matter that is decaying, or breaking down.

You may have heard the terms '**predator**' and 'prey'. A predator is an animal that eats another animal. The prey is the animal that is eaten. Food chains include both predators and prey.

Can an animal be both predator and prey? Yes. An animal might have two different roles in a food chain. Sometimes it might be a predator and eat smaller animals. But it might become prey when an animal higher up on the food chain eats it. One animal can have a place in several food chains.

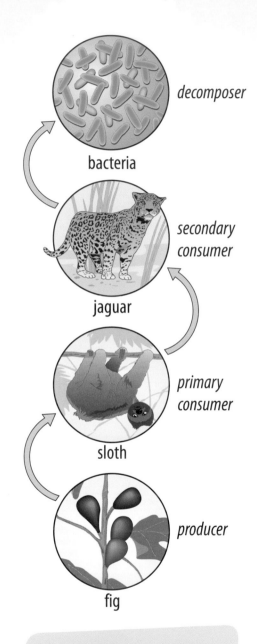

decomposer

bacteria

secondary consumer

jaguar

primary consumer

sloth

producer

fig

Energy in this food chain begins with a producer (fig) and ends with a decomposer (bacteria).

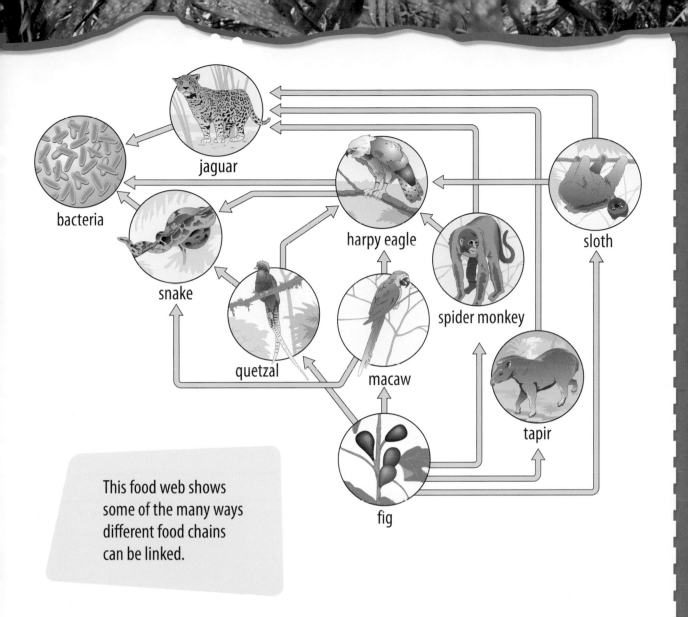

jaguar

bacteria

snake

quetzal

harpy eagle

macaw

spider monkey

sloth

tapir

fig

This food web shows some of the many ways different food chains can be linked.

WHAT IS A FOOD WEB?

Food chains only tell one part of the story. They show one series of links. Many organisms eat more than one type of organism. This is a good idea for survival. Animals that eat only one thing are at risk if something happens to their food source.

A food web shows how food chains are linked together. It looks a bit like a spider web. A food web shows how energy moves from organism to organism. It tells you who eats whom. In the food web above, figs are food for both tapirs and macaws.

WHAT IS A RAINFOREST HABITAT?

Rainforests are warm areas of dense **vegetation** and heavy rain. The hot, moist conditions support many different **species** (types) of plants and animals. You can find rainforests in **tropical** areas all over the world. The largest rainforests are in South America around the River Amazon, in Africa around the Congo and Niger rivers, and in India and Southeast Asia. Australia, the Philippines, and Papua New Guinea also have small rainforests.

The rainforest is an amazing place to live. It is very warm all year around. The temperature usually stays between 20°C (68°F) and 32°C (90°F). Within each rainforest are many different **habitats**. A habitat is a place where **organisms** of the same kind live. Organisms depend on their habitat for food, shelter, water, and everything else they need to survive.

The Korup National Rainforest in Cameroon sustains a wide variety of organisms.

Red and blue macaws rest on the branch of a rainforest tree.

The top layer of the rainforest is called the **canopy**. It is a dense group of treetops, forming a blanket of leaves. Sometimes, the canopy is so dense it does not allow sunlight to get through. Below the canopy, the **understory** is alive with climbing animals, tangling vines, and flowering orchids. On the forest floor, deer **graze**, army ants march, and ferns and mosses grow.

All living things are **adapted** to their habitat. If a plant lives in the canopy and needs lots of sunlight, then it is adapted to the canopy. It probably would not survive on the forest floor. Over time organisms develop **adaptations** that help them to survive in certain habitats.

WHERE IN THE WORLD ARE RAINFOREST HABITATS?

The map below shows the location of the world's rainforests.

NORTH AMERICA

Central American rainforest

Amazon rainforest

SOUTH AMERICA

ASIA

EUROPE

AFRICA

south-eastern Asian
rainforests

Indian
rainforest

African
rainforest

AUSTRALIA

Australian
rainforest

ANTARCTICA

WHAT ARE THE PRODUCERS IN RAINFORESTS?

Producers, or plants, turn **energy** from the Sun into food. This process is called **photosynthesis**.

All producers need sunlight, water, carbon dioxide, and **nutrients** to grow. Plants contain **chlorophyll**, a substance that makes them green. Chlorophyll is made of protein that helps plants trap sunlight to use in photosynthesis.

Producers are very important. All **consumers** depend on producers in some way. Some consumers eat producers. Some eat other consumers that eat producers. If the producers disappeared, the consumers would, too. It would affect the entire food chain.

PLANT LAYERS

Producers live at different layers of the rainforest. Tall evergreen trees reach 23 to 30 metres (75 to 100 feet) to form the **canopy**. That is about as high as 13 to 16 people standing on each other's shoulders. Some very tall trees poke through this high canopy. This is called the **emergent layer**.

Below the canopy is the **understory**. This is where smaller trees, plants, and shrubs grow. On the forest floor is a layer of ferns, mosses, and herbs.

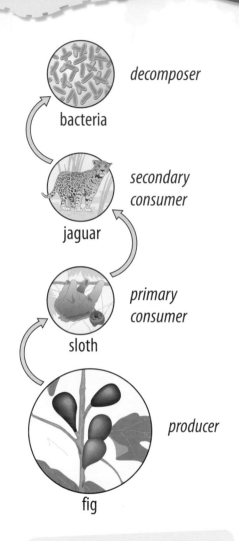

decomposer
bacteria

secondary consumer
jaguar

primary consumer
sloth

producer
fig

Producers, such as the fig, get energy from the Sun before being eaten by a consumer.

STRANGLER FIGS

Some plants have unusual ways of taking in nutrients. Strangler figs are able to draw out nutrients from trees. Wind blows strangler fig seeds onto a treetop. From its treetop perch, it grows roots down the tree. These roots take in nutrients from the tree. Eventually, a strangler fig kills its host tree by squeezing its trunk and sucking out all of its nutrients.

The strangler fig's roots take in nutrients from the tree it grows on.

WHAT PLANTS CAN BE FOUND IN RAINFORESTS?

Rainforest soil does not contain many nutrients. Plants **adapt** to get nutrients from ground plants that die and decay. The dead matter settles in the top layer of soil. Trees and plants take in these nutrients through shallow roots.

Thick green or woody vines are a common sight in the rainforest. Vines are plants that attach to other plants. They climb up trees to catch the sunlight. But vines also serve another function. Monkeys and orangutans use them to travel from tree to tree!

A bromeliad's waxy leaves are good at trapping water.

AIR PLANTS

Some of the most unusual rainforest plants are **epiphytes**. Epiphytes are air plants that have adapted to living above the soil. They grow on tree trunks or branches. But they do not take in nutrients from the tree. They absorb nutrients straight from the air and rain water. Epiphytes include mosses, lichens, orchids, ferns, and bromeliads.

Orchids and bromeliads bring bursts of colour to the rainforest. Many orchids have striking, colourful blooms. Bromeliads' thick, waxy leaves form a bowl to collect water. Sometimes insects or tiny frogs live in this pool of water!

LOSING A LINK: HEALING PLANTS

The Amazon rainforest has tens of thousands of plant **species**. Some of these plants can be used as medicine. There are rainforest plants that cure malaria and some that help fight cancer. Many of these special plants cannot be found anywhere else in the world. Scientists believe many species of healing plant have not been discovered yet. But **habitat** loss is putting these species at risk. Many are dying out before scientists have a chance to find them. When species die out, we lose chances to save lives.

Bark from the cinchona tree can be used to make a medicine that fights malaria.

WHAT ARE THE PRIMARY CONSUMERS IN RAINFORESTS?

Any **organism** above the level of **producer** is a **consumer**. Consumers cannot make their own food. They feed on producers or other consumers. Right above the producers in the food chain are the **primary** (first) **consumers**. Primary consumers feed on producers. They are **herbivores**, or plant-eaters.

Many different primary consumers live in the rainforest. There is a wide range of plant **species** to support them. Some organisms remain in the **canopy** for their entire lives. Others remain on the forest floor. Rainforest primary consumers include insects, butterflies, birds, and rodents.

REMARKABLE RODENTS

One of the largest rainforest rodents is the agouti. Agoutis look like large guinea pigs. They have coarse, oily hair, small ears, and a stumpy tail. They live in burrows or hollow tree trunks and eat fallen fruit and nuts.

The world's largest rodent is the capybara. This pig-like creature has shaggy, reddish-brown fur. It lives in South America and grows up to 60 centimetres (2 feet) tall. Capybaras feed mainly on grasses, water plants, and fruit. Sometimes they eat their own **faeces** (poo)! The poo contains **bacteria** that help break down tough plant material in the capybara's stomach.

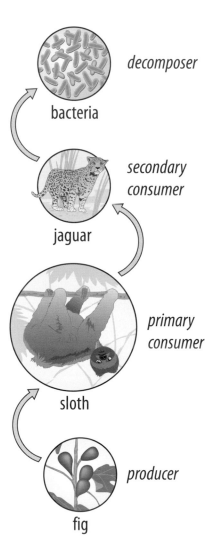

decomposer

bacteria

secondary consumer

jaguar

primary consumer

sloth

producer

fig

The sloth, a primary consumer, feeds on figs, a producer.

Rainforest ants climb an acacia plant. The ants live in the hollow thorns.

SLOW AS A SLOTH

The three-toed sloth lives in Central and South America. It clings to trees with its clawed feet. It moves so slowly that algae grows on its shaggy fur. This helps it blend in with rainforest **vegetation** and avoid **predators**. The three-toed sloth sleeps for up to 20 hours a day. Leaves and twigs make up its diet.

PERFECT PARTNERS

Ants have a special relationship with the acacia plant. Hollow acacia thorns provide shelter and food for ants and their young. The ants, in turn, protect the acacia from organisms that try to eat it.

WINGS IN THE RAINFOREST

Many flying creatures make their homes in the rainforest. These include bats, birds, and butterflies.

BATS

Fruit bats are an important part of the rainforest food chain. Some plants depend on the bat for **pollination** (fertilization). When a bat drinks **nectar** from a flower, it also **pollinates** the flower.

BIRDS

The rainforest is alive with bird sounds. Toucans boast colourful beaks and black-and-yellow bodies. They eat fruit, insects, small lizards, and eggs. They warm up or cool down their beaks to control their body temperature.

Noisy parrots live in rainforests around the world. They fly from treetop to treetop in the canopy and **emergent layer**. Their sharp beaks break apart nuts, seeds, and fruits.

Hummingbirds are the smallest birds on Earth. They beat their wings so fast you can barely see them. They hover in mid-air and dip their long beaks into the sweet nectar of a flower, sucking it up with their long tongues.

A hummingbird feeds on sweet nectar in mid-air.

BUTTERFLIES

More species of butterfly live in the rainforest than anywhere else. The Amazon rainforest alone contains 7,500 species.

The blue morpho butterfly has striking blue wings. The wings are not actually coloured blue. Tiny scales on top of the wings reflect blue light, making them appear blue. With its wings closed, the dull brown underside shows. This makes it hard for predators, such as birds, to see it. Adult blue morphos sip tree sap and fruit juice.

Scales on top of the blue morpho butterfly's wings reflect blue light.

A BROKEN CHAIN: FRUIT BATS

In Queensland, Australia, fruit bats are at risk. Because of **habitat** loss, they cannot find enough **pollen** and nectar from their usual plant sources. So they head lower into the **understory** to eat wild tobacco berries. But this plant is home to a deadly tick that has killed many bats. Without fruit bats to pollinate them, many rainforest plants could die out.

WHAT ARE THE SECONDARY CONSUMERS IN RAINFORESTS?

Secondary consumers feed on **primary consumers**. These **predators** hunt and eat other animals.

GROUND PREDATORS

Rainforest ground predators include snakes, lizards, and small **mammals** such as bandicoots and coatimundi. Mammals are furry, warm-blooded animals that produce milk to feed their young.

Most rainforest snakes are small to medium in size and **prey** on insects, birds, and small mammals. The giant anaconda can grow up to 9 metres (30 feet) long. Found in South America and Trinidad, it is one of the world's largest snakes. These big snakes eat a wide range of animals, including deer, turtles, fish, and birds.

Australian bandicoots have long, pointed noses like rodents, but are not rodents. They forage at night for worms, spiders, insects, and plant roots. Bandicoots nest on the ground or in hollow logs.

The coatimundi are related to raccoons. They have thick fur and use a long tail for balance. Coatimundis search for food on the forest floor and in the **understory**. They are **omnivores**. They eat scorpions, spiders, lizards, rodents, and small mammals. They also eat fruit. In fact, coatis eat just about anything!

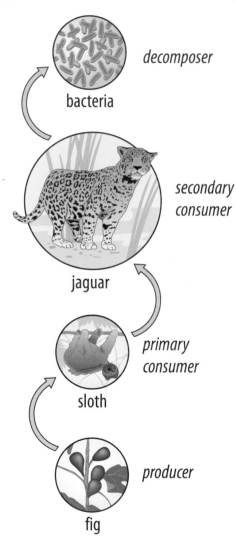

decomposer

bacteria

secondary consumer

jaguar

primary consumer

sloth

producer

fig

The jaguar, a secondary consumer, eats primary consumers such as a sloth.

Not all snakes stick to slithering. Snakes such as this Chrysopelea appear to fly when they glide through the air.

FLYING PREDATORS

Some predators have special **adaptations** to get from tree to tree. They look as if they fly, but they do not have wings. Insect-eating frogs use webbed feet to glide short distances between trees. Flying snakes of the Southeast Asian rainforest glide from tree to tree in search of their prey – mostly birds, bats, rodents, and lizards. The flying dragon is a rainforest lizard that eats insects. It stretches its skin so that it can sail between trees up to 8 metres (25 feet) apart.

TOP RAINFOREST CONSUMERS

The rainforest food web contains many **primate species**. Primates are a group of mammals that share certain features. They have hands that grasp and well-formed brains. Monkeys and gorillas are primates. So are humans. Some primates are primary consumers, and some are secondary consumers. Both chimpanzees and mandrills are secondary consumers.

Chimpanzees are humans' closest relatives. Like humans, they are omnivores. They eat fruits and vegetables and some animals, including insects, monkeys, and pigs. Chimps can use tools. They poke long sticks and branches into termites' nests to get at these tasty snacks.

Shy monkey-like mandrills are difficult to spot in the wild. They live in **tropical** African rainforests. Mandrills eat reptiles and insects as well as roots and fruits. They live in groups, and the males have colourful faces.

Chimpanzees use twigs to dig into trees for termites.

TOP RAINFOREST PREDATORS

Do any creatures feed on secondary consumers? Yes. These are the top predators in rainforest food chains. They are fearsome **carnivores**. Some people call them **tertiary consumers**, meaning 'third-level **consumers**'.

The top rainforest predators are the 'big cats', such as jaguars and ocelots. Fierce jaguars prey on tapirs, monkeys, tortoises, and birds. Ocelots are not very big – about twice the size of a pet cat – but they are good hunters. Their sharp teeth tear into rabbits, rodents, frogs, and other small animals.

MOST DANGEROUS PREDATOR

Another top predator is . . . you! Humans have hunted big cats almost to **extinction**. In some parts of the world, people hunt and eat chimpanzees and other primates. Laws are in place to protect these animals, but some people ignore the laws.

An ocelot is on the prowl for prey.

LOSING A LINK: BIG CATS IN DANGER

Top predators need large ranges (areas of land to hunt in). As rainforest **habitat** disappears, it is harder for the big cats to survive. Many are now **endangered** (at risk of dying out).

WHAT ARE THE DECOMPOSERS IN RAINFORESTS?

Decomposers are an important link in rainforest food chains. They play a key role in the cycle of life and death. Decomposers break down dead plant and animal matter. This frees up **nutrients** for the beginning of the chain. Then, rainforest **producers** consume these nutrients and the food chain begins again.

This process is a bit like recycling. When we put out glass bottles to be recycled, the glass can be used again to make other things. When decomposers break down matter, it can be used again. This is especially important in the rainforest, where the soil is poor. Plants take in nutrients directly from decaying matter.

Without decomposers, the waste would build up and up and up. Soon the entire rainforest would be filled with dead matter.

In this food chain, a decomposer (bacteria) breaks down the body of a **secondary consumer** (jaguar).

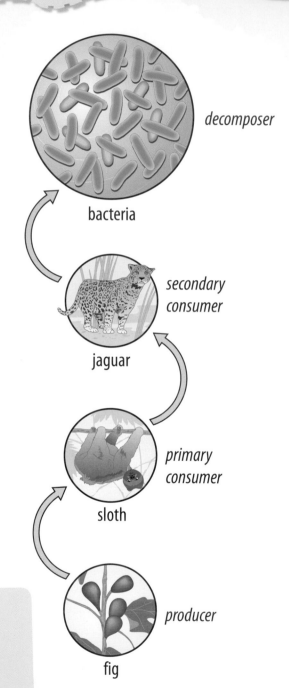

decomposer

bacteria

secondary consumer

jaguar

primary consumer

sloth

producer

fig

A king vulture feeds on
a dead armadillo.

SCAVENGER HUNT

Scavengers begin the process of breaking down dead matter. Termites help to break down fallen trees and branches. Worms go to work on dead plants and animals. Dung beetles eat rotting fruit and leaves as well as **faeces**.

King vultures are the bird world's largest scavengers. They soar above the **canopy** looking for dead animals to feast on. The vulture's yucky diet might help out in another way. Eating rotting animal flesh might help stop the spread of disease.

Long trails of leaf-cutter ants are a common sight in rainforests. These ants do not actually feed on leaves. They feed on a **fungus** that grows on piled-up leaf material. They cut up leaves into smaller pieces to bring back to their colony. There, the fungus breaks down the leaf pieces. Leaf-cutter ants are very strong. They can carry leaf pieces 20 times their weight. A person who could do that would be able to lift a small car!

BREAKING IT DOWN

Rainforests are areas with a high temperature and a lot of moisture. This helps plant matter break down quickly. Dead plants and animals can break down in as little as 24 hours if the rainforest is hot and moist enough. In other places, it can take far longer for dead material to break down. **Bacteria** and fungi complete the process of breaking down dead matter.

LOSING A LINK: FROG-KILLING FUNGUS

Most fungi are important rainforest decomposers. But one type of chytrid fungus is killing frogs in Australia and Central America. The fungus causes a deadly skin disease in some frogs. Many frogs have died out, and many more are at risk. Most types of chytrid fungus help break down plant matter. Scientists are not sure why one type became harmful to frogs.

This frog is being tested for a deadly fungus.

BENEFICIAL BACTERIA

Bacteria are the main rainforest decomposers. These are very simple but important **organisms**. Bacteria are single-celled organisms. (Cells are the smallest units of living things.) Some bacteria are shaped like rods, and others like spirals.

Bacteria are tiny. You could fit about a million of them on the head of a pin. Bacteria help break down dead matter into substances other organisms can use. Some bacteria live everywhere, including the digestive systems of rainforest organisms, helping them to break down food. Other bacteria live on faeces and help to break it down.

FUNGUS AMONG US

Another important decomposer is fungus. Mushrooms are a common type of fungus. They grow especially well in warm, wet rainforests. Bracket fungi grow directly on dying or dead trees. They look like ladders attached to a tree trunk. Some fungi come in strange shapes. An earthstar puffball fungus looks like a puffy flower with spiky 'petals'.

These fungi act as decomposers of this dead rainforest tree.

WHAT ARE RAINFOREST FOOD CHAINS LIKE AROUND THE WORLD?

Rainforest **habitats** share many features, but they are not all the same. **Species adapt** to their specific habitat. Rainforest food chains differ from one part of the world to another.

THE AMAZON RAINFOREST

The River Amazon **basin** is home to the largest rainforest in the world. It stretches from Peru to eastern Brazil. The area contains almost half of the **tropical** rainforest habitat left in the world.

Nearly 40,000 plant species have been found here. The Amazon rainforest also boasts the most species of bird, butterfly, and freshwater fish on Earth.

A two-toed sloth rests on a branch in Costa Rica.

This pygmy marmoset lives in the trees in a rainforest in Brazil.

Jaguars prowl the forest floor looking for **prey**. Harpy eagles swoop down and tear into reptiles sunning themselves on rocks. Two-toed sloths blend in with the dense **vegetation**. Colourful scarlet macaws squawk from treetop perches.

Primates such as marmosets live in the lush **understory** of the Amazon. Tiny pygmy marmosets are the world's smallest monkeys. They grow to only 13 centimetres (5 inches) long. Marmosets feed on lizards, spiders, and insects as well as tree sap and fruit.

Poison dart frogs have a unique defence against **predators**. The colourful frogs release toxins (poison) from their skin. Predators that try to gobble up poison dart frogs get a painful – and sometimes deadly – surprise.

A BROKEN CHAIN: LOSING THE AMAZON

The Amazon is an important part of the planet. It is home to plants that can treat disease and save lives. Many animals found here cannot survive anywhere else. But the Amazon rainforest is disappearing. Farmers cut down and burn the edges of the rainforests to make room for crops and animals. Scientists say that more than half of the Amazon rainforest could be gone by 2030. Many plants and animals here are at risk of dying out.

THE AFRICAN RAINFOREST

The African rainforest is the second largest in the world. It follows the path of Africa's River Congo. Half of all the animal species in Africa live in the rainforest.

Many of the **producers** here have practical uses. Coffee plants grow in the shade of tall trees. Local people harvest the pods of cacao trees to make chocolate. Wood from tall mahogany trees is used to make furniture and flooring. African oil palms produce oil for soap, chocolate, and other products.

The African rainforest is home to many primates, including lowland gorillas, chimpanzees, and bonobos. Bonobos, like chimps, are close relatives of humans. They feed on fruits, nuts, mushrooms, and sometimes even rodents or small antelope. Bonobos are found in the Congo and nowhere else on Earth.

Other rainforest **mammals** include forest elephants, hippopotamuses, and okapi. The okapi, a relative of the giraffe, lives only in the African rainforest. Okapis eat fruits, plants, and **fungi**. African elephants are one of the world's largest land animals. Adults eat up to 136 kilograms (300 pounds) of roots, fruits, grass, and bark each day.

This food chain shows one way plants and animals are consumed in the African rainforest.

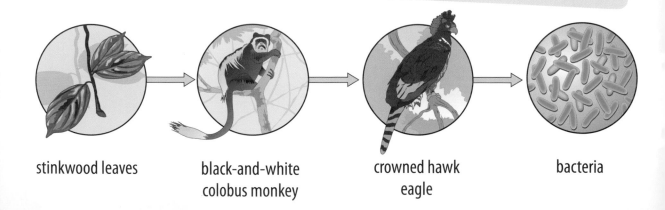

stinkwood leaves   black-and-white colobus monkey   crowned hawk eagle   bacteria

A chimpanzee crouches in the West African rainforest.

LOSING A LINK: DISAPPEARING RAINFORESTS

The African rainforest is disappearing – and along with it many primate species. Farming and road building are wiping out vast areas of land. Despite laws against it, some people still hunt and eat primates. About 90 per cent of the African rainforest is gone already. What will happen to the primates?

GENTLE GIANTS

You might assume gorillas are tough predators. Think again. These powerful creatures look fierce but are actually quite gentle. They only strike out when threatened. Gorillas are mostly **herbivores** that eat leaves, shoots, and fruits.

SOUTHEAST ASIAN RAINFOREST

In Southeast Asia, you will find the oldest rainforests in the world. These rainforests are not large expanses like those of the Amazon and Congo river basins. Thailand, Malaysia, and Myanmar (Burma) have smaller areas of rainforest. Sumatra, Borneo, New Guinea, and the Philippines also contain patches of rainforest. This is because the landscape contains many islands and because of human development.

All plants are producers. But some plants are also **secondary consumers**, or **carnivores**! Pitcher plants have bowl-shaped parts that trap insects or other animals. The insect falls in or is lured in by sweet **nectar**. Then the pitcher plant takes in **nutrients** from the dead insect. Some pitcher plants in Southeast Asia lure in animals as large as rats!

Orangutans swing through the jungles of Sumatra and Borneo. These shaggy, red-haired apes spend most of their time in the understory. They munch on fruit, nuts, and bark. Sometimes birds' eggs or termites make tasty snacks for orangutans. About 50,000 orangutans remain in the wild. They are at risk of dying out.

Small lemurs live only on the island of Madagascar. They live in the trees and use their long, furry tails for balance. Some lemurs eat insects, while most eat leaves and fruit.

This food chain links organisms in the Southeast Asian rainforest.

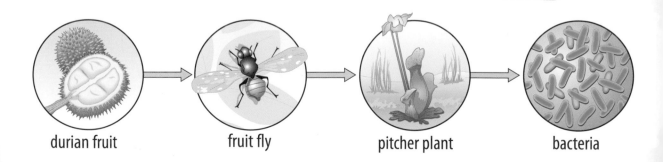

durian fruit   fruit fly   pitcher plant   bacteria

A BROKEN CHAIN: BORNEO

The island of Borneo, which is around three times the size of the United Kingdom, is home to an amazing number of species. About 15,000 species of plant are found here. Borneo's rainforest is the world's tallest. Many 'flying' animals, from frogs and lizards to snakes and squirrels, fling themselves from tree to tree. Today, less than half of Borneo's rainforest remains. Forest fires, logging, and farming have destroyed much of this unique habitat.

This Wallace's flying frog is found in the rainforest of the island of Borneo.

All over the world, rainforest food chains are in trouble. Human activity has already wiped out half of Earth's rainforests. Rainforests once covered 14 per cent of Earth. Now they cover only 6 per cent. Yet the rainforest is still home to half the **species** on Earth.

Why should we protect these special **habitats**? Rainforests house many rare plant and animal species. Many rainforest **organisms** cannot be found anywhere else on Earth. Some plant species can help to treat or cure disease. When these species disappear, we lose chances to save lives.

LUNGS OF THE EARTH

Rainforests are like the lungs of the planet. They give off oxygen that humans and other animals need to breathe. They also act as a 'carbon sink'. Rainforest **vegetation** absorbs carbon dioxide gas. Otherwise, carbon dioxide would build up and trap heat, creating **global warming**. Global warming puts many species, including humans, at risk.

Rainforest plants absorb carbon dioxide and give off oxygen.

Burning can destroy areas of rainforest.

HABITAT LOSS

From South America to Southeast Asia, rainforests are disappearing fast. Every minute, an area of rainforest the size of 50 football fields disappears.

Logging, farming, road building, and wars have led to widespread habitat loss. Cities and towns have taken over land that was once rainforest.

Clear-cutting is a farming practice in which land is cleared completely. This process destroys **native** plant species. Another damaging practice is slash-and-burn farming. First, farmers harvest whatever wood they can. Then, they burn the rest of the land to make way for crops or **grazing** animals.

All these activities end up killing plants and forcing animals to find new homes. But where will these animals go? They are pushed into smaller and smaller areas of land. There, they must compete for fewer resources.

RAINFORESTS AT RISK

Many rainforests are at risk from mining. Rainforests contain many substances that are valuable to humans, such as gold, copper, and nickel. But mining operations release lots of waste. This harmful waste **pollutes** the air and water. It can harm – or even kill – plants and animals living nearby. The effects of **pollution** last for a long time. It can be difficult, or even impossible, to clean up polluted land.

A BROKEN CHAIN: SAPO NATIONAL PARK

One area at risk from mining and hunting is Sapo National Park. This park is in the African country of Liberia. It is the second largest rainforest in West Africa. But there are not enough park rangers to protect the park. People illegally hunt forest elephants and pygmy hippopotamus there. They clear the forest for grazing cattle and for growing crops. Some mine for gold and diamonds in the park. Many species that live in Sapo National Park are in danger, including chimpanzees and colobus monkeys.

Mines such as this one are responsible for polluting and destroying rainforests.

Humans can pass on diseases to primates such as gorillas.

DISAPPEARING PRIMATES

Hunting threatens many rainforest species. **Primates** such as chimps and lowland gorilla are now **endangered**. Fewer than 100,000 chimpanzees remain in the world. There are between 172,000 and 300,000 lowland gorillas, the type of gorilla that lives in **tropical** rainforests.

In parts of Africa, people illegally hunt primates for food. Their flesh is called 'bushmeat'. The growth of towns and tourism also can affect the health of gorillas. People who come into contact with gorillas can pass on diseases to them.

Primates are our closest living relatives. Humans have much to learn from them. If they die out, we will lose a valuable link to our history.

A small area of rainforest was cleared for this cattle pasture.

HOPE FOR THE FUTURE

What will happen to the rainforests? Their fate is in human hands.

There is some good news. In some places, the rainforest is growing back. About 350,000 square kilometres (135,000 square miles) of rainforest is growing back around the world. Scientists have noted that the **canopy** fills in after about 15 years. This gives hope for the future.

The regrowth is due mainly to changing patterns of human life. In places such as Panama and parts of the Congo, more people are moving into cities. They are leaving behind farms grown on former rainforest land.

On these empty patches of land, the rainforest is taking over once more. Dense vegetation is filling in spaces where cattle once grazed or coffee once grew. Birds and other creatures are making a new home in this habitat.

But the new rainforest is not the same as it once was. The species that have died out can never come back. Old-growth rainforests (ones with very old trees) take in more carbon dioxide and give off more oxygen than regrown forests. Because of this, they are better at slowing global warming.

Still, it is hopeful news. More land means hope for many rainforest plants and animals. If the new rainforest is to thrive and grow, people must protect it. The future of the rainforests is up to us.

MADE IN THE RAINFOREST

The rainforest is home to many plants with practical uses. These plants make our lives easier, tastier, and more fun. Rubber, Brazil nuts, coffee, chocolate, cinnamon, and vanilla are just a few rainforest products. Think about what life would be like without those things.

Parts of the Bunya Mountains rainforest in Queensland, Australia that were once logged have regrown.

WHAT CAN YOU DO TO PROTECT RAINFOREST FOOD CHAINS?

The rainforest supplies oxygen to the planet. It is home to many amazing **species** of plant and animal. If you or someone you love gets ill, rainforest plants might provide a treatment or cure. Today, the rainforest needs your help. What can you do to help protect it?

SUPPORT CONSERVATION GROUPS

People all over the world are working to preserve the rainforest. Support **conservation** groups that put money and research towards the problems facing the rainforest. Groups like the World Wildlife Fund work hard every day to prevent illegal hunting, fishing, and farming in the rainforest.

This zoo worker tries to give medicine to a sick orangutan that was illegally smuggled out of a rainforest.

It is important to support people who live in or near rainforests.

HELP ALL RAINFOREST DWELLERS

Hippopotamuses and tapirs are not the only creatures that dwell in the rainforest. People make their home there, too. Millions of people across the world depend on rainforests for food and shelter. Sometimes these people do not have enough to eat. This drives them to hunt **endangered** animals or to chop down forests to grow crops or **graze** animals. It is important to help the people of the rainforest, too. Without their help, the rainforests will not survive.

FUEL FROM FUNGUS?

Petrol is a major source of **pollution**. But it is hard to find a substitute. Now scientists have discovered one substance that might work. A type of tree **fungus** can turn plant matter into fuel. The fungus grows in the rainforests of Patagonia, at the tip of South America. Scientists think this might be a good source of renewable **energy**. Renewable energy is clean fuel from sources that do not run out, such as sunshine or wind. The fungus could grow in labs or in factories. It may help reduce our dependence on petrol.

CHILDREN CAN MAKE A DIFFERENCE

In Manuel Antonio, Costa Rica, children are working together to protect the rainforest. Kids Saving the Rainforest is a conservation group founded by two schoolchildren. In 1998, two nine-year-old girls decided to sell painted rocks to raise money for the local rainforest. More than 10 years later, the group is still going strong.

Today, the organization works to preserve rainforests and save endangered local monkeys. Kids Saving the Rainforest built an animal shelter to care for injured animals. The group releases the healthy animals back into the wild. Pupils who volunteer with the group help build monkey bridges. These bridges are built across roads in Manuel Antonio. They help local monkeys cross the road without getting hit by cars.

Children around the world can get involved in the group by raising money or asking local businesses to sponsor a monkey or rainforest tree.

Cards and letters from children in support of the Children's Eternal Rainforest in Costa Rica are displayed. This rainforest reserve is completely supported by children!

BUY SUSTAINABLE AND FAIRTRADE PRODUCTS

Ask your parents to buy rainforest products – such as bananas, chocolate, and coffee – that are grown sustainably. **Sustainable** products are grown in a way that does not harm the rainforest. Also, ask your parents to make sure that your furniture and flooring is made from sustainable wood. Look for wood from certified sustainable forests.

Another label to look for is 'fairtrade'. Fairtrade products are made in ways that are less harmful to the environment. Fairtrade also means that the person who buys or grows the product is paid a fair price.

SPREAD THE WORD

Learn as much as you can about the amazing plants and creatures that live in the rainforest and take steps to protect them. Then share your knowledge with people you know. Together we can make a difference!

This woman harvests a fairtrade coffee crop. It is important to buy fairtrade products when possible.

TOP 10 THINGS YOU CAN DO TO PROTECT RAINFORESTS

There are lots of things you can do to protect rainforest food chains and **habitats**. Here are 10 to get you started:

1 Reduce, reuse, and recycle. Save trees. Use as little paper as possible. When you use paper, make sure it is recycled.

2 Write a letter to a **conservation** group to thank it for what it does. Or write to a group harming the rainforest and ask it to stop.

3 Hold a cake sale or raffle to raise money for conservation groups such as the World Wildlife Fund, or the Rainforest Conservation Fund.

4 Ask your parents to buy sustainably-grown rainforest products. **Sustainable** products are grown or produced in ways that do not harm rainforests.

5 Buy **organic** food, if possible. **Pesticide** use harms rainforests and habitats everywhere.

6 At home or on holiday, don't feed wild animals. Animals **adapt** to their habitat. Feeding them human food disrupts their diet and could make them ill.

7 Let wild animals stay wild. Don't buy rainforest fish, monkeys, or birds to keep as pets. These animals belong in the rainforest. They are a key part of the rainforest food chain.

8 Support the people who live in the rainforest. They need your help, too! They depend on the rainforest for food and shelter.

9 Learn as much as you can about rainforests. Tell your friends and family what you have learned.

10 Write an article in your school newspaper telling people how they can protect rainforests.

GLOSSARY

adapt develop a feature that helps a living thing survive. If a plant lives in the rainforest understory, then it is adapted to low levels of sunlight.

adaptation feature that helps a living thing survive. The poison that some frogs release from their skin is an adaptation that helps them scare off predators.

bacteria simple, one-celled living things. Bacteria help break down dead matter in the rainforest.

basin dip in the land

canopy top layer of the rainforest formed by treetops clustered together. Tall evergreen trees reaching up to 30 metres (100 feet) high form the canopy.

carnivore animal that eats only other animals. Jaguars and ocelots are the main rainforest carnivores.

chlorophyll chemical that makes plants green and helps them trap sunlight.

clear-cutting removal of all trees in an area

conservation preserving something, such as a natural resource. Some conservation groups help protect the rainforest.

consumer animal that cannot make its own food. Consumers eat plants or other animals, or both plants and animals.

decomposer living thing that breaks down dead plant and animal matter. Bacteria are the main rainforest decomposers.

emergent layer very tall trees that poke through the rainforest canopy. The emergent layer is above the canopy.

endangered at risk of dying out. Chimpanzees and lowland gorillas are endangered.

energy power needed to grow, move, and live

epiphyte plant that grows on tree trunks or branches and absorbs (takes in) nutrients from rain water and air. Orchids, ferns, and bromeliads are all epiphytes.

extinction when all living things of a certain kind die out. Jaguars and ocelots are at risk of extinction.

faeces solid waste from an animal (poo)

fungus (plural: **fungi**) group of rainforest decomposers that includes mushrooms. Fungus grows quickly in warm, wet rainforests.

global warming worldwide increase in air and ocean temperature. The loss of rainforest will worsen global warming.

graze eat grass and other green plants in a field or meadow

habitat place where organisms of the same kind live. Living things are adapted to their habitat.

herbivore living thing that eats only plants. Gorillas are rainforest herbivores.

mammal warm-blooded animal that produces milk to feed its young. Rats, gorillas, and humans are all mammals.

GLOSSARY

native plant or animal that lives in the place it is adapted to

nectar sugary substance made by plants

nutrient substance a living thing needs to live or grow

omnivore animal that eats both plants and animals. Humans are omnivores.

organic made in a natural way or containing only natural materials

organism living thing

pesticide poisonous chemical used to kill insects and other pests

photosynthesis process plants use to turn sunlight into energy

pollen small grains that are the male part of a flower

pollinate fertilize a plant by transferring pollen from another plant

pollination when a plant is fertilized by transferring pollen from another plant

pollute release harmful waste into the land, air, or water

pollution harmful waste

predator animal that eats another animal

prey animal that is eaten by another animal; also, when an animal pursues another animal to eat it

primary consumer animal that consumes producers (plants)

primate group of mammals that share certain features, such as hands that grasp and large brains for their body size. Monkeys, gorillas, chimpanzees, and humans are all primates.

producer organism that can make its own food, using energy from the Sun. Plants are producers.

scavenger animal that feeds on dead matter

secondary consumer predator, or animal that feeds on a primary consumer

species type of plant or animal. Rainforests are home to thousands of plant and animal species.

sustainable something that is done in a way that does not use up resources. Sustainable products are raised or produced in a way that does not harm the environment.

tertiary consumer third-level consumer, or animal that feeds on animals that eat other animals. 'Big cats' are the top tertiary consumers.

tropical having to do with a region of high temperatures and heavy rainfall. Rainforests are found in tropical areas of the world.

understory area below the canopy in a rainforest. Smaller trees, plants, and shrubs grow in the understory.

vegetation plant life. Rainforests contain many kinds of vegetation.

FIND OUT MORE

BOOKS

100 Facts on Rainforests, Camilla de la Bedoyere (Miles Kelly Publishing Ltd, 2009)

How Can We Save Our World? Sustainable Rainforests, Anne Rooney (Franklin Watts, 2009)

Planet Earth: Rainforests, Steve Parker (QED Publishing, 2009)

Protecting Habitats: Rainforests in Danger, Moira Butterfield (Franklin Watts, 2008)

The Vanishing Rainforest, Richard Platt (Frances Lincoln Publishers, 2007)

WEBSITES

www.rainforest-alliance.org/education
Visit the website of the Rainforest Alliance for fun facts, stories, and projects dealing with the plants and animals of the rainforest.

www.kidssavingtherainforest.org
Kids Saving the Rainforest, a not-for-profit group based in Costa Rica, links pupils with rainforest conservation projects.

www.rainforestconcern.org/tour/rfc_guide.htm
Rainforest Concern runs this website, where Jessie the Jaguar will take you on a virtual tour of the rainforest and its plants, animals, and sounds.

schools.rainforestsos.org/kids
The Prince's Rainforests Project for Schools website includes factsheets, short videos, photos rainforest sounds, games and activities, and ideas for saving the rainforests.

FURTHER RESEARCH

Choose a topic from this book you'd like to research further. Do you live near a rainforest you would like to know more about? Or is there a faraway rainforest you think is exotic? Was there a creature in this book you find interesting? Is there something harming rainforest food chains you'd like to know more about putting a stop to? Visit your local library to find out more information.

INDEX